MW01245773

Oh, The Places God Wants to Take You

Amy Junod

TRILOGY CHRISTIAN PUBLISHERS

Tustin, CA

Trilogy Christian Publishers
A Wholly Owned Subsidary of Trinity Broadcasting Network
2442 Michelle Drive
Tustin, CA 92780

Oh, The Places God Wants to Take You

Copyright © 2024 by (Amy Junod)

Scripture quotations marked NJKV are taken from the New King James Version®. Copyright © 1982 by Thomas Nelson. Used by permission. All rights reserved.

Scripture quotations marked MSG are taken from *THE MESSAGE*, copyright © 1993, 2002, 2018 by Eugene H. Peterson. Used by permission of NavPress. All rights reserved. Represented by Tyndale House Publishers, Inc.

All rights reserved, including the right to reproduce this book or portions thereof in any form whatsoever.

For information, address Trilogy Christian Publishing

Rights Department, 2442 Michelle Drive, Tustin, CA 92780.

Trilogy Christian Publishing/ TBN and colophon are trademarks of Trinity Broadcasting Network.

For information about special discounts for bulk purchases, please contact Trilogy Christian Publishing.

Trilogy Disclaimer: The views and content expressed in this book are those of the author and may not necessarily reflect the views and doctrine of Trilogy Christian Publishing or the Trinity Broadcasting Network.

10 9 8 7 6 5 4 3 2 1

Library of Congress Cataloging-in-Publication Data is available.

ISBN 979-8-89333-769-3

ISBN 979-8-89333-770-9 (ebook)

Contents

Introduction

God gave us everything on Earth to enjoy on the surface, but everything given to us also has deeper meaning.

Early in 2023, God gave me a vision as I was watching a news program. The program was discussing Christian revival breaking out in schools around the country. This is what I saw: lines of color in frames, similar to what you'd see at an art museum or gallery. There were two paintings, both similar in their design, but each with different colors like a flag.

The colors in the paintings were given to you-this generation, to help you sort out what God means...what He is saying to you as you begin your journey with Him through life. Seek God, and you will find Him.

Author's note: All Scripture is taken from the New King James Bible except otherwise noted.

Colors: What Do They Mean to God?

Let the stubbornness of the world be removed from you and let the fire of God consume you.

Move away from disease of this life, and move toward holiness as the bride of Christ.

The blue balloon represents leaving behind worldly situations and taking off in a new life with God.

You are moving from sin and death into God's mysteries.

Revelation and communion with God will come from Heaven to you.

As you turn toward God's light, you will have growth in Him, with abundance in life.

Turn toward the light of God and walk in His purity.

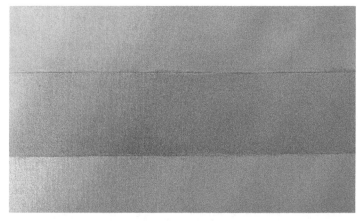

The colors of the rainbow are not the colors of worldly pride, rather they are the colors of God's promise.

The rainbow is a symbol of God's faithfulness and mercy.

The word "pride" means to have too high an opinion of one's own ability or worth. Pride is a feeling of being better than others.

The word "promise" means to assure someone that one will definitely do, give, or arrange something; the colors of the rainbow are not the color of pride, rather, they are the colors of God's promises to you.

"Pride" says the color red means life and passion.

"Promise" says the color red represents the blood that Jesus shed when He was on the cross, for the forgiveness of our sins so that we may be healed. God's promise is the strongest form of love!

"Pride" says the color orange means healing, fun, and celebration.

"Promise" says the color orange is the fire of God--being in God's presence or Holiness.

"Pride" says the color yellow represents sunlight, radiance, and a bright future.

"Promise" says the color yellow represents God's joy and His anointing.

"Pride" says the color green represents nature, prosperity, and growth.

"Promise" says that green symbolizes everlasting life, growth in God, fruitfulness, and God's grace for you.

"Pride" does not acknowledge the color blue.

"Promise" says the color blue relates to peace and knowledge of God, as well as the mercy of God.

"Pride" says indigo represents serenity, calmness, and relaxation.

"Promise" says indigo symbolizes God's heavenly grace.

"Pride" says violet represents spirit, royalty, and superiority.

"Promise" says violet represents spiritual wisdom, and also reflects God's attention to our sorrow and suffering.

In Genesis, God talks about rainbows as a sign of His mercy.

The rainbow also represents a covenant made to Noah that God would never flood the Earth again. You will find the story of Noah in Genesis, chapters six through ten.

> "Like the appearance of a rainbow in a cloud on a rainy day, so was the appearance of the brightness all around it. This was the appearance of the likeness of the glory of the LORD. So when I saw it, I fell on my face, and I heard a voice of One speaking."
>
> (Ezekiel 1:28)

In this verse, rainbows are compared to the glory of God!

The Bible also talks about rainbows in the book of Revelation. John, the author, likens the glory or presence of God to a rainbow.

> "Immediately I was in the Spirit; and behold, a throne set in heaven, and One sat on the throne. And He who sat there was like a jasper and a sardius stone in appearance; and there was a rainbow around the throne, in appearance like an emerald."
>
> (Revelation 4:2-3)

What's next?

Let's look at one of the Bible's most well-known verses:

> "For God so loved the world that He gave His only begotten Son, that whoever believes in Him should not perish but have everlasting life."
>
> (John 3:16)

Most of us have read or memorized this verse, but what does it really mean? Is there more to it than what we think at first? Please read the same verse and the proceeding verse in the Message translation:

> This is how much God loved the world: He gave his Son, his one and only Son. And this is why: so that no one need be destroyed; by believing in him, anyone can have a whole and lasting life. God didn't go to all the trouble of sending his son merely to point an accusing finger, telling the world how bad it was. He came to help, to put the world right again. Anyone who trusts in him is acquitted; anyone who refuses to trust Him has long since been under the death sentence without knowing it. And why? Because of that person's failure to

believe in the one-of-a-kind Son of God when introduced to him." This is the crisis we're in: God-light steamed into the world, but men and women everywhere ran for the darkness. They went for the darkness because they were not really interested in pleasing God. Everyone who makes a practice of doing evil, addicted to denial and illusion, hates God-light and won't come near it, fearing a painful exposure.

But anyone working and living in truth and reality welcomes God-light so the work can be seen for the God-work it is.

John 3:16-21 (MSG)

Salvation is simply acknowledging the need to be saved from sin by asking Jesus Christ to come into your heart.

The Journey of Asking Jesus into Your Heart: The Romans Road

"As it is written: "There is no one righteous, no, not one."

(Romans 3:10)

The point of this verse is every single person has messed up or sinned in some way.

"But God demonstrates His own toward us, in that while we were still sinners, Christ died for us."

(Romans 5:8.)

God, Jesus, and the Holy Spirit came up with a plan before God created the world, that Jesus would come to Earth and die for our sins!

"...That if you confess with your mouth the Lord Jesus and believe in your heart that God has raised Him from the dead, you will be saved. For with the heart one believes unto righteousness, and with the mouth confession is made unto salvation."

(Romans 10:9-10)

"For 'whoever shall call upon the name of the Lord shall be saved.'"

(Romans 10:13)

If this is the desire of your heart, a prayer like the one below needs to be prayed:

Dear Jesus, I believe that you died on the cross for my sins. I understand I am a sinner and need to be saved. You are the only way this can happen. Please come into my heart and forgive my sins. Amen.

Welcome to the family!

"And the Spirit and the bride say, "Come!' And let him who hears say, "Come!" And let him who thirsts come. Whoever desires, let him take the water of life freely."

(Revelation 22:17)

The following areas are very important to your Christian walk.

Soul and Spirit

What is your soul and spirit? How do they work?

Your soul is your mind, emotion, and will. The soul understands this world. It's the knowledge in your head. It's the five senses; touch, sight, hearing, smell, and taste. God gave us these to use in this world.

> "And the LORD God formed man of the dust of the ground, and breathed into his nostrils the breath of life; and man became a living being."
>
> (Genesis 2:7)

> "Then the dust will return to the earth as it was, and the spirit will return to God who gave it."
>
> (Ecclesiastes 12:7)

> "Behold, all souls are Mine; The soul of the father as well as the soul of the son is Mine; The soul who sins shall die."
>
> (Ezekiel 18:4)

"And do not fear those who kill the body but cannot kill the soul. But rather fear Him who is able to destroy both soul and body in hell,"
(Matthew 10:28)

The spirit is what understands the things of God. The spirit understands the truths of the Bible. The spirit seeks God to understand what He wants for our life. The spirit of a person is also known as your heart.

"For what man knows the things of a man except the spirit of the man which is in him? Even so no one knows the things of God except the Spirit of God."
(1 Corinthians 2:11)

"The Spirit Himself bears witness with our spirit that we are children of God..."
(Romans 8:16)

"But there is a spirit in man, and the breath of the Almighty, gives him understanding."
(Job 32:8)

Prayer

The meaning of prayer is a devout petition to God; a spiritual communion with God, as in supplication, thanksgiving, adoration, or confession.

In Matthew 6:9-13 Jesus teaches us how to pray. It reads:

> "In this manner, therefore pray: Our Father in heaven, hallowed be Your name. Your kingdom come. Your will be done on earth as it is in heaven. Give us this day our daily bread. And forgive us our debts, as we forgive our debtors. And do not lead us into temptation, but deliver us from the evil one. For Yours is the kingdom and the power and the glory forever. Amen."

Jesus gave us this prayer to model our prayers after. As we pray, our prayers are placed into bowls and placed before the throne of God.

> "Now when He had taken the scroll, the four living creatures and the twenty-four elders

fell down before the Lamb, each having a harp, and golden bowls full of incense, which are the prayers of the saints."

(Revelation 5:8)

What happens to the prayer bowls? Do they just become incense before God? What's the purpose?

Revelation 8:3-5 says:

"Then another angel, having a golden censer, came and stood at the altar. He was given much incense, that he should offer it with the prayers of all the saints upon the golden altar which was before the throne And the smoke of the incense, with the prayers of the saints, ascended before God from the angel's hand. Then the angel took the censer, filled it with fire from the altar, and threw it to the earth. And there were noises, thunderings, lightnings, and an earthquake."

God answers our prayers when the bowl of prayer is full. Some answers may be instant; others can take years. Don't quit praying. Don't give up.

Here are several more scriptures on prayer:

"Ask, and it will be given to you; seek, and you will find; knock, and it will be opened to you. For everyone who asks receives, and he who seeks finds, and to him who knocks it will be opened."

(Matthew 7:7-8)

"Now this is the confidence that we have in Him, that if we ask anything according to His will, He hears us. And if we know that He hears us, whatever we ask, we know thar we have the petitions that we have asked of Him."

(1 John 5:14-15)

"But you, when you pray, go into your room, and when you have shut your door, pray to your Father who is in the secret place; and your Father who sees in secret will reward you openly. And when you pray, do not use vain repetitions as the heathen do. For they think that they will be heard for their many words."

(Matthew 6:6-7)

"He shall call upon me, and I will answer him...."

(Psalms 91:15)

"Call to Me, and I will answer you, and show you great and mighty things, which you do not know."

(Jeremiah 33:3)

"...That the God of our Lord Jesus Christ, the Father of glory, may give to you the spirit of wisdom and revelation in the knowledge of Him."

(Ephesians 1:17)

For this reason we also, since the day we heard it, do not cease to pray for you, and to ask that you may be filled with the knowledge of His will in all wisdom and spiritual understanding;
that you may walk worthy of the Lord, fully pleasing Him, being fruitful in every good work and increasing the knowledge of God strengthened with all might, according to His glorious power, for all patience and longsuffering with joy; giving thanks to the Father who has qualified to be partakers of the inheritance of the saints in the light.

(Colossians 1:9-12)

Forgiveness

You also need to know that asking for forgiveness is important. A lack of forgiveness toward others means that the Lord will not forgive us. Learning forgiveness is not just about being able to ask your Heavenly Father for forgiveness, but also being able to ask forgiveness of those who were wronged and hurt by your actions and words. It is also important to forgive others for wrongs they have done to you. The following are scriptures regarding forgiveness:

> "For if you forgive men their trespasses, your heavenly Father will also forgive you. But if you do not forgive men their trespasses, neither will your Father forgive your trespasses."
> (Matthew 6:14-15)

> But love your enemies, do good, and lend, hoping for nothing in return; and your reward will be great, and you will be sons of the Most High. For He is kind to the unthankful and evil.

Therefore be merciful, just as your Father also is merciful. Judge not, and you shall not be judged. Condemn not, and you shall not be condemned. Forgive, and you will be forgiven.

(Luke 6:35-37)

"Do not say, "I will recompense evil"; wait for the LORD, and He will save you."

(Proverbs 20:22)

Mark 11:22-26 talks about forgiveness and how it works with faith. It reads:

"So Jesus answered and said to them, "Have faith in God. For assuredly, I say to you, whoever says to this mountain, 'Be removed and be cast into the sea', and does not doubt in his heart, but believes that those things he says will be done, he will have whatever he says. Therefore I say to you, whatever things you ask when you pray, believe that you receive them, and you will have them. And whenever you stand praying, if you have anything against anyone, forgive him, that your Father in heaven may also forgive you your trespasses. But if you do not forgive, neither will your Father in heaven forgive your trespasses."

You always have to be practicing forgiveness...for everything, all the time. Never hold a grudge against anyone, otherwise, you won't be able to move forward in your faith and walk with God.

Faith

Faith can be stated as standing in complete contrast to doubt due to the lack of tangible proof. This means having a strong belief in something, regardless of not having tangible proof.

Hebrews 11 is considered the faith chapter. It reviews some of the Old Testament greats that displayed great faith.

> "Now faith is the substance of things we hoped for, the evidence of things not seen."
>
> (Hebrews 11:1)

> "But without faith it is impossible to please Him, for he who comes to God must believe that He is, and that He is the rewarder of those who diligently seek Him."
>
> (Hebrews 11:6)

> "But you, beloved, building yourselves up on your most holy faith, praying in the Holy

Spirit, keep yourselves in the love of God,
looking for the mercy of the Lord Jesus Christ
unto eternal life."

(Jude 1:20-21)

That the genuineness of your faith, being
much more precious than gold that perishes,
though it is tested by fire, may be found to
praise, honor, and glory at the revelation of
Jesus Christ, whom having not seen you love.
Though now you do not see Him, yet believ-
ing, you rejoice with joy inexpressible and full
of glory, receiving the end of your faith—the
salvation of your souls.

(1 Peter 1:7-9)

Love

There's four different types of love.

"Storge" love is a family love that you have for family relationships.

> "Husbands, love your wives, just as Christ also loved the church and gave Himself for her."
>
> (Ephesians 5:25)

"Phileo" refers to love between friends.

> "Be kindly affectionate to one another with brotherly love, in honor giving preference to one another."
>
> (Romans 12:10)1

> "Let brotherly love continue."
>
> (Hebrews 13:1)

"Eros" love is a passion love.

> "I am my beloved's, and my beloved is mine..."
>
> (Song of Solomon 6:3)

Flee sexual immorality. Every sin a man does is outside the body, but he who commits sexual immorality sins against his own body. Or do you not know that your body is the temple of the Holy Spirit who is in you, whom you have from God, and you are not your own? For you were bought at a price, therefore glorify God in your body and in your spirit, which are God's."

(1 Corinthians 6 18-20)

"*Agape*" love is God's love for us.

Matthew 5:43-46 reads:

"You have heard that it was said, 'You shall love your neighbor and hate your enemy.' But I say to you, love your enemies, bless those who curse you, do good to those who hate you, and pray for those who spitefully use you and persecute you, that you may be sons of your Father in heaven; for He makes His sun rise on the evil and on the good and sends rain on the just and on the unjust.

For if you love those who love you, what reward have you? Do not even the tax collectors do the same?"

Matthew 22:37-39 tells us:

> "Jesus said to him, "You shall love the LORD Your God with all your heart, with all your soul, and with all your mind."
> This is the first and great commandment.
> And the second is like it: "You shall love your neighbor as yourself.""

> "And we have known and believed the love that God has for us. God is love, and he who abides in love abides in God, and God abides in him."
>
> (1 John 4:16)

1 Corinthians, chapter thirteen, is the love chapter of the Bible. Here is a guideline for how we are doing with love. 1 Corinthians 13:4-8 says:

> "Love suffers long and is kind; love does not envy; love does not parade itself, it is not puffed up; does not behave rudely, does not seek its own, is not provoked, thinks no evil; does not rejoice in iniquity, but rejoices in the truth; bears all things, believes all things, hopes all things, endures all things. Love never fails..."

How will you and the people who know you know that you follow Jesus? Following Jesus is seen in the way you act, talk, in the games you play, the movies you watch, and the places you go.

I say then: Walk in the Spirit, and you shall not fulfill the lust of the flesh. For the flesh lusts against the Spirit, and the Spirit against the flesh; and these are contrary to one another, so that you do not do the things you wish. But if you are led by the Spirit, you are not under the law.

Now the works of the flesh are evident, which are: adultery, fornication, uncleanness, lewdness,

idolatry, sorcery, hatred, contentions, jealousies, outbursts of wrath, selfish ambitions, dissensions, heresies, envy, murders, drunkenness, revelries, and the like; of which I tell you beforehand, just as I also told you in time past, that those who practice such things will not inherit the Kingdom of God. But the fruit of the Spirit is love, joy, peace, longsuffering, kindness, goodness, faithfulness, gentleness, self-control. Against such there is no law. And those who are Christ's have crucified the flesh with its passions and desires. If we live in the Spirit, let us also walk in the Spirit. Let us not become conceited, provoking one another, envying one another.

(Galatians 5:16-26)

"For those who live according to the flesh set their minds on things of the flesh, but those who live according to the Spirit, the things of the Spirit."

(Romans 8:5)

"For this reason we also, since the day we heard it, do not cease to pray for you, and to ask that you may be filled with the knowledge of His will in all wisdom and spiritual understanding;
that you may walk worthy of the Lord, fully pleasing Him, being fruitful in every good work and increasing in the knowledge of God."

(Colossians 1:9-10)

You might have heard of the Ten Commandments. Those are still important to those who follow Christ, even today. They are found in Exodus 20:1-17. The Commandments are also reviewed several times in the first few books of the Bible, some of which go into more detail.

> "I am the LORD your God...You shall have no
> other gods before Me."
>
> (Exodus 20:2-3)

(In Biblical times, idols were made of stone, wood, or metal. Today, idols are whatever is more important in your life than God.)

> "You shall not make for yourself a carved image—any likeness of anything that is in heaven above, or that is in earth beneath, or that is in the water under the earth; you shall not bow down to them nor serve them..."
>
> (Exodus 20:4-5)

(Do not create any idols, whether they be figurative in your heart, or literal. You should not worship or value anything above God.)

> "You shall not take the name of the LORD your God in vain, for the LORD will not hold him guiltless who takes His name in vain."
>
> (Exodus 20:7)1

(Do not take God's name in vain. He will hold you accountable for this. This means that you should not be saying phrases like "Oh, God!" or "Oh. My God!". Remember to not use Jesus' name as a swear word.

Speaking cleanly is important when following the Ten
Commandments.)

"Remember the Sabbath day, to keep it holy."

(Exodus 20:8)

(Take one day of the week and set it aside to rest. Go to
church and honor God with praise and worship! Don't
forget to spend time with your friends and family. God
will then bless the other six days, so you can get everything accomplished that is needed in life during those
times)

"Honor your father and your mother..."

(Exodus 20:12)

(If you honor and obey your parents, God will give you
a long, prosperous life.)

"You shall not murder."

(Exodus 20:13)

(You should not commit this sin, be it literally or in the
sense of hating someone in your heart. Forgive everyone, always, as Jesus forgave you!)

"You shall not commit adultery."

(Exodus 20:14)

(If she is not your missus, or if he is not your mister, hands off! Do the right thing; honor God, marriage, and the person. Wait until you are married.)

> "You shall not steal."
>
> (Exodus 20:15)

(Don't even think about it...)

> "You shall not bear false witness against your neighbor."
>
> (Exodus 20:16)

(There's no need to lie about anything. The truth sets you free from sin and guilt.)

> "You shall not covet... anything that is your neighbor's."
>
> (Exodus 20:17)

(Don't spend time wanting what other people have. Be content with all God gives you. If you are truly God's, He is all you need.)

Baptism

Being baptized by water means that you are being immersed in water. This symbolizes the idea that your sins are washed away and you are a new person in Jesus.

"He who believes and is baptized will be saved; but he who does not believe will be condemned."

(Mark 16:16)

"Go therefore and make disciples of all the nations, baptizing them in the name of the Father and of the Son and of the Holy Spirit, teaching them to observe all things that I have commanded you; and lo, I am with you always, even to the end of the age. Amen."

(Matthew 28:19-20)

For Christ also suffered once for sins, the just for the unjust, that He might bring us to God, being put to death in the flesh but made alive by the Spirit, by whom also He went and preached to the spirits in prison, who were formerly disobedient, where once the Divine longsuffering waited in the days of Noah, while the ark was being prepared, in which a few, that is, eight souls, were saved through water. There is also an antitype which now saves us–baptism (not the removal of the filth of the flesh, but the answer of a good conscience toward God), through the resurrection of Jesus Christ,

who has gone into heaven and is at the right hand of God, angels and authorities and powers having been made subject to Him.

(1 Peter 3:18-22)

There is also baptism by fire, or baptism of the Holy Spirit. For this baptism, it is not an act of doing, but of seeking and desiring a deeper relationship with God through the Holy Spirit.

When the Day of Pentecost had fully come, they were all with one accord in one place. And suddenly there came a sound from heaven, as of a rushing mighty wind, and it filled the whole house where they were sitting. Then there appeared to them divided tongues, as of fire, and one sat upon each of them. Then they were all filled with the Holy Spirit and

began speaking with other tongues, as the
Spirit gave them utterance.

(Acts 2:2-4)

Likewise the Spirit also helps in our weak-
nesses. For we do not know what we should
pray for as we ought, but the Spirit Himself makes intercession for us with groan-
ings which cannot be uttered. Now He who
searches the hearts knows what the mind of
the Spirit is, because He makes intercession
for the saints according to the will of God.

(Romans 8:26-27)

The Armor of God

God has provided us with very important body armor. It serves to protect us as we go through our life. We need to put this armor on daily. Sometimes, we need to put it on many times throughout the day. Don't leave your bed without it! Your armor is found in Ephesians 6:10-20:

> "Finally, my brethren, be strong in the Lord and the power of His might.
>
> Put on the whole armor of God, that you may be able to stand against the wiles of the devil.
>
> For we do not wrestle against flesh and blood, but against principalities, against powers, against rulers of the darkness of this age, against spiritual hosts of wickedness in the heavenly places. Therefore take up the whole armor of God, that you may be able to withstand in the evil day, and having done all, to stand. Stand, therefore, having girded your

waist with truth, having put on the breast-plate of righteousness, and having shod your feet with the preparation of the gospel of peace; above all, taking up the shield of faith with which you will be able to quench all the fiery darts of the wicked one. And take the helmet of salvation, and the sword of the Spirit, which is the word of God; praying always with all prayer and supplication in the Spirit, being watchful to this end with all perseverance and supplication for all the saints--and for me, that utterance may be given to me, that I may open my mouth boldly to make known the mystery of the gospel, for which I am an ambassador in chains; that in it I may speak boldly, as I ought to speak."

I also found these little nuggets that I thought would be beneficial for everyone;

"I have restrained my feet from the evil way, that I may keep Your word."

(Psalms 119:101)

"How sweet are Your words to my taste, sweeter than honey to my mouth."

(Psalms 119:103)

"Your word is a lamp to my feet and a light to my path."

(Psalms 119:105)

According to the Armor of God, we are instructed to shod our feet with the preparation of the gospel of peace. If you look at Psalm 119 again, you'll see that God's word is a lamp to our feet. So, the more we are in the Word, the more we apply it to our lives, the more our lives will have peace in them!

Now, what about armor for your backside?

Isaiah states this about your rear guard:

"Then your light shall break forth like the morning, your healing shall spring forth speedily, and your righteousness shall go before you; The glory of the LORD shall be your rear guard."

(Isaiah 58:8)

What is the glory of the Lord? This is the manifestation of holiness, magnificence, majesty, the beauty, splendor, brilliance, and praise of God.

Then Moses went up into the mountain, and a cloud covered the mountain. Now the glory of the LORD rested on Mount Sinai, and the

cloud covered it six days. And on the seventh
day He called Moses out of the midst of the
cloud. The sight of the glory of the Lord was
like a consuming fire on the top of the mountain in the eyes of the children of Israel.

(Exodus 24:15-17)

John 11:40 tells us:

"Jesus said to her, "Did I not say to you that if
you would believe you would see the glory of
God?""

1 Corinthians 10:31 says:

"Therefore, whether you eat or drink, or whatever you do, do all to the glory of God."

We need to make sure that whatever we are doing
brings glory to God. How we speak, how we treat others, what we watch on tv, and who we associate with
should all strive to bring Him glory.

"Arise, shine; For your light has come! And
the glory of the Lord is risen upon you."
(Isaiah 60:1)

So, people around you should notice a difference in
you. Most people's countenance changes, they become

brighter and lighter in the face after accepting Jesus into their heart. That is because the glory of the Lord changes you visibly.

Gifts

God, Jesus, and the Holy Spirit love us so much that they gave us gifts. These gifts are not only for us individually, but also for us to share with others! You may not receive the entire list from each, but you will receive at least one from each. Also, you may realize one gift has been in your life all along.

Gifts from God:

> And God has appointed these in the church: first apostles, second prophets, third teachers, after that miracles, then gifts of healings, helps, administrations, varieties of tongues. Are all apostles? Are all prophets? Are all teachers? Are all workers of miracles? Do all have gifts of healing? Do all speak with tongues? Do all interpret? But earnestly desire the best gifts. And yet I show you a more excellent way.
>
> 1 Corinthians 12:28-31

Gifts from Jesus:

> "He who descended is also the One who ascended far above all heavens, that He might fill all things. And He Himself gave some to be apostles, some prophets, some evangelists, and some pastors and teachers..."
>
> (Ephesians 4:10-11)

Here's some explanation for what the above are:

Apostles set proper order and foundation. They launch people into ministry. They guard and protect the church and the territory that they are assigned to. They are revelatory in their gifting capacity. They generally build up and teach to send people into their gifting and calling.

Prophets are revelatory. They hear God. They are concerned with having a proper foundation, proper order, rank, and file. They're interested in disturbing the status quo to continue moving into the present truth that is being revealed, which is revelation from God.

Pastors are shepherds. They nurture, protect, teach, and feed. They watch over the flock. They are not so much revelatory, even though they receive revelation from God.

Evangelists are the ones that go out and spread the gospel. They have a burning desire to release the knowledge of the gospel. They want to share the power of God through salvation with people.

Teachers teach and learn line upon line to instruct. They gain insight and revelation. They take what the prophets and apostles are saying and instruct others so that they may learn from it.

Gifts of the Holy Spirit:

But the manifestation of the Spirit is given to each one for the profit of all:

> for to one is given the word of wisdom through the Spirit, to another the word of knowledge through the same Spirit, to another faith by the same Spirit, to another gifts of healing by the same Spirit, to another the working of miracles, to another prophecy, to another discerning of spirits, to another different kinds of tongues, to another the interpretation of tongues. But one and the same Spirit works all these things, distributing to each one individually as He wills.
>
> (1 Corinthians 12:7-11)

What is the best gift? The best gift is what is needed at the moment. It is very important to be able to flow in all the gifts mentioned in the previous three sets of verses. However, you will notice that some gifts are stronger in your life than others.

The Names of God

Well, you serve a new to you, God! What is His name? What do his names mean? His many names reveal a characteristic He has. There are hundreds of names and titles for God. I will give a short list here, just to get you started:

"Yaweh": "I Am"

> Then Moses said to God, "Indeed, when I come to the children of Israel and say to them, 'The God of your fathers has sent me to you,' and they say to me, 'What is His name?' what shall I say to them?" And God said to Moses, "I AM WHO I AM." And He said, "Thus you shall say to the children of Israel, 'I AM has sent me to you.'" Moreover, God said to Moses, "Thus you shall say to the children of Israel: 'The LORD God of your fathers, the God of Abraham, the God of Isaac, and the God of Jacob, has sent me to you. This is My name forever, and this is My memorial to all generations.
>
> (Exodus 3:13-15)

"Jehovah Rapha"—God that Heals or Restores

> "And said, 'If you diligently heed the voice
> of the LORD your God and do what is right
> in His sight, give ear to His commandments
> and keep all His statutes, I will put none of
> the diseases on you which I have brought on
> the Egyptians. For I Am the LORD who heals
> you.'"
>
> (Exodus 15:26)

"Elohim"—The Creator

> "In the beginning God created the heavens
> and the earth."
>
> (Genesis 1:1)

"El Shaddi"—God Almighty

> "And God spoke to Moses and said to him:
> 'I am the LORD I appeared to Abraham, to
> Isaac, and to Jacob, as God Almighty, but by
> My name LORD I was not known to them.'"
>
> (Exodus 6:2-3)

"Jehovah Jireh"—God Will Provide

> "And Abraham called the name of the place
> The-LORD-Will-Provide; as it is said to this

day, "In the Mount of the LORD it shall be provided."

(Genesis 22:14)

"Adonai"—My Lord, He Will Manifest "Hear, O Israel: The LORD your God, the LORD is One!'

You shall love the LORD your God with all your heart, with all your soul, and with all your strength. And these words which I command you today shall be in your heart. You shall teach them diligently to your children and shall talk of them when you sit in your house, when you walk by the way, when you lie down, and when you rise up. You shall bind them as a sign on your hand, and they shall be as frontlets between your eyes. You shall write them on the doorposts of your house and on your gates.

(Deuteronomy 6:4-9)

Books of the Bible

There are sixty-six books in the Bible. The Old Testament is made up of thirty-nine, and the New Testament has twenty-seven books. Here is a list of the books of the Bible, and what you can expect to find in them in order as they were written.

Old Testament

Law: Genesis, Exodus, Leviticus, Numbers, Deuteronomy

History: Joshua, Judges, Ruth, 1 Samuel, 2 Samuel, 1 Kings, 2 Kings,1 Chronicles, 2 Chronicles, Ezra, Nehemiah, Esther

Wisdom: Job, Psalms, Proverbs, Ecclesiastes, Song of Song

Prophets: Isaiah, Jeremiah, Lamentations, Ezekiel, Daniel, Hosea, Joel, Amos, Obadiah, Jonah, Micah, Nahum, Habakkuk, Zephaniah, Haggai, Zechariah, Malachi

New Testament

Gospels: Matthew, Mark, Luke, John

Church History: Acts

Paul's Letters: Romans, 1 Corinthians,
2 Corinthians, Galatians, Ephesians,
Philippians, Colossians, 1 Thessalonians,
2 Thessalonians, 1 Timothy, 2 Timothy,
Titus, Philemon

General Letters: Hebrews, James, 1 Peter,
2 Peter, 1 John, 2 John, 3 John, Jude

Prophecy: Revelation

That's a lot of books to read through, but you can do it! Try starting with the gospels. I suggest reading the book of John first, then reading the rest of the gospels. You will learn about the life of Christ through these. I also suggest reading a Proverb each day. There are enough Proverbs for you to read one chapter each day of the month. By reading these Proverbs over and over, you will gain knowledge and wisdom. If you read five Psalms a day, you will get through the book in a month. While reading Psalms, you will learn the heart of King David and others toward God. Reading four chapters daily will get you through the entire Bible in one year. However, it is also good to take your time and meditate on verses, asking the Holy Spirit to help you to understand them fully. This is especially important for the words in the New Testament.

Keeping a journal of your walk with God is helpful. It's important to write out what you are learning in the scriptures. Writing out prayer requests and answers to past prayers are essential, too. You may also have dreams that you won't want to forget. Maybe you will feel God talking to you. It is important to write that out. Sometimes, doing a study on words found in the Bible, in someone's life, or in a verse could also be part of a journal. Let the Holy Spirit guide you in how and what to journal.

Church

And let us consider one another order to stir up love and good works, not forsaking the assembly of ourselves together, as is the manner of some, but exhorting one another, and so much the more as you see the Day approaching.

(Hebrews 10:24-25)

What to look for in a church:

- Does the church believe in God, Jesus, and the Holy Spirit?
- Does the church believe in the entirety of the Bible?
- Do they believe that it is the same yesterday, today, and forever?
- Does the church believe in the gifts of God, Jesus, and the Holy Spirit?
- Are they in flowing in these gifts in the church?

- Does the church believe that it is important to have knowledge of what is going on in the world, and to represent Christ well?

Printed in the USA
CPSIA information can be obtained
at www.ICGtesting.com
LVHW021124221024
794500LV00001B/7